TOTAL Sh*T

An Excremental Essay About President Trump

by Paul Orwell

Total Sh*t: An Excremental Essay About President Trump

Table Of Contents

Author's Note

A *Shittery* Is At The Back Of This Book!

I believe words matter. For most people, words (mainly hot air) come out of their mouths while shit comes out the other end, but Trump has it all ass-backwards.

Our president talks a lot of shit and this book talks a lot of shit about our president — there's so much shit flying around that I've included a helpful lexicon at the back of the book called *The Shittery*. Throughout the book, when you see a shitty word or phrase in brown that's underlined, like weird shit, flip to *The Shittery* at the back to look up its meaning. Inhale, shit-daddle to the back now, and hold your breath until the Mueller madness has died down...then again, you'll be dead. You can reach me at paul@paulorwell.com. I am at paulorwelll (that's a one on the end) on Twitter, and my website is https://paulorwell.tumblr.com/

Preface: Shit Storm

In this short book, I look at Donnie Trump through the lens of excrement because he is, in a sense, the physical embodiment of our nation's collective shit. My hope is that this quick splash of his fecal treacle will help you to diagnostically, politically, and culturally orient to this new reality, and I include a lexicon of useful phrases called *The Shittery at the back.* They'll help you navigate the Trumpocracy we live in and assess his presidency which has, since day one, been diarrhetic, and has now developed into a full-blown public health crisis I call Trumpoma.

* * *

I grew up in dairy country, surrounded by farmland. One of my most vivid childhood memories is driving behind a manure spreader carrying a full load. As it lumbered down the narrow rural road, little lumps of shit tumbled onto the pavement and the stench of cow effluent wafted into the car. Even with the windows closed, the putrid odor sneaked in, crept up my nose, and raked the back of my throat.

Suddenly, the manure spreader veered hard right into a field and the farmer yanked the rear discharge lever. As the spreader's large spiral beaters began twisting in opposite directions, their blades pulverized the fertilizer and expelled it forcibly while the farmer drove slowly across the pasture. It was quite literally a shitstorm: excrement flying everywhere and coating everything.

Today we live in a shitstorm called the Trump Presidency. It covers everyone and everything in filth, flies, and lies. Instead of Donnie doing his job and fertilizing the soil of democracy to make America great again, his crap blights the land, leaving it depleted, despoiled, and defiled. We are choked by Barr's ammonia now breezing around Capitol Hill and the White House. We need to re-plow and replant or else we'll start retching.

This book is a Declaration of Elimination. A primal scream that dreams of finally being free of the sounds and smells of the putrid mass of this two-hundred-and-sixty-six-pound shit that streams interminable excrement over your TV, radio, and to the internet like manure. So much has been written about Donald Trump — it seems like a book is published for every single news cycle — that we've become (mostly) immune to the allegations and apologies. This book offers none of the above. Hopefully, you don't Barr-f. Its purpose is simple and Mueller-like: to help you satisfy the urge to purge.

My point of view on Donald Trump is that he is a total and unadulterated shit. A pestilence. He talks shit, tweets shit, eats shit, excretes shit, and is a conceited shit-for-brains president who treats everyone like shit.

Just so you understand where I am coming from.

Eat Shit

Let's talk coprophagia. The word means, literally, to eat shit. It's what we do here in America right now. We are fed Trump's shit and we simply gobble it down. It's depressing. We haven't been in this much shit since the Great Horse Manure Crisis of 1894. In those days, trade and transportation relied on beasts of burden, leaving the world's capitals quite literally buried in millions of pounds of manure, with citizens poisoned by the stench, pestilence, and disease that accompanied it.

Back then, it took 100,000 horses each shitting over 20 pounds daily to suffocate New York City. Today, one man, encouraged by his voting base, has left this nation drowning in shit. In the process, Donnie has left shit stains on the United States Constitution, the U.S. court system, and has laid waste to the American dream. It is our duty to flush him out of our systems — but we must look before we flush, because analyzing Trump's dumps will help us to dump Trump.

What goes into our bodies as food takes a slow cruise down to the anal canal, transforming from fuel to stool, from table to toilet, from the mouth south. The end result — a rear discharge of water and waste — is a veritable gravy train of riches that reveals much about our health and well-being. It's a view into the rumblings, grumblings, and fumblings that take place in the belly of the beast.

In addition to meaning "feces", a "shit" is defined as a contemptible or worthless person, or it can be an exclamation of disgust, anger, or annoyance, like "Oh Shit!" Our president is a contemptible shit, physically and metaphorically speaking.

We'll use the Bristol Stool Scale, developed at the Bristol Royal Infirmary, as a turd guide to Donnie's daily shitload. Created by medical professionals, this diagnostic tool describes and illustrates seven primary types of poos, which range from constipation (types 1 and 2), through normal (types 3 and 4), to increasingly severe diarrhea (types 5 to 7).

Type 1: Separate hard lumps, like nuts (hard to pass)

This type of shit stews in the colon for days. Something's rotten in the state of Trump's bowels — often it's nuts like Nancy Pelosi, Jeff Sessions, or whomever else happens to be on Donnie's daily shit list. Call this one the Constitutional Crisis: Though his gut rages with sound and fury, Trump's puny poops signify nothing, thus ruining his morning constitutionals.

Type 2: Sausage-shaped but lumpy

If a Type 2 poo had a face, it would look like Steve Bannon's. If it were a Trump product, it might be a cowboy bone-in ribeye from his now-defunct steak brand. It's large, it's in charge, it's as monumental as the Titanic or Trump Tower, and it's so painful it's akin to giving birth. Senior officials within earshot have code-named this crap Give Me Liberty, Or Give Me Death based on the faint cries Trump makes while performing this intolerable act.

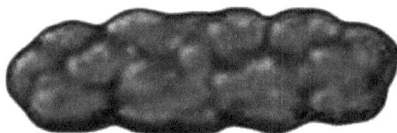

Type 3: A sausage shape with cracks in the surface

Leaving constipation territory and entering the evacuation zone, the #3 is like an all-American hotdog with its casing split (situation's normal, all fucked up). Trump likens his to Lincoln Logs and threatens to build the wall with them should more traditional methods fail to support. Attorney General Bar is a #3.

Type 4: Long and smooth like a snake

Always a smooth operator, Trump boasts
his #4s are very tremendous turds, as "long
and beautiful" as he claims his fingers to
be. They're the gold standard of shits, a
masterpiece of merde, the champion of craps.
Truth or alternative fact? A reasonable
facsimile of his shit can be found at the
official Trump Store online. The Trump
Gold Bullion Chocolate Bars sold there are,
according to one Ohio couple, "just regular
chocolate" but with a "good, thick waxy
feel."

Type 5: Soft blobs with clear-cut edges (passed easily)

Small shit-biscuits shaped like chicken nuggets or tater tots. Donnie likes to give these female names based on whose breasts they resemble and has been known to remark, apropos of nothing, "not bad, just squeezed out a couple of O'Donnells" to any unfortunates paid to listen to his crap. It is thought that many of his tweets are little more than veiled references to when Donnie makes a number five.

Type 6: Fluffy pieces with ragged edges, a mushy stool

Normally Donnie drinks half a dozen 12-ounce Diet Cokes a day. Once he hits one hundred ounces, those in his inner circle recognize it as an unmistakable sign of the madness to come. His shits tend to develop

uneven edges as the carbon dioxide
sublimates out of the stool, giving them the
consistency of soft-serve ice cream or lumpy
gravy. Donnie refers to them as "hokey
cokeys"; pundits and proctologists have
posited that the reason the erstwhile
Republican candidate once "snorted his way
through" debates was because he was trying
to hold in his sixes.

**Type 7: Watery, no solid pieces. Entirely
liquid.**

Open the floodgates, there's an epic
shitstorm a brewin'. Donnie is a big fan of
police water cannons but does not like them
coming out of his anus. As brown liquid
(colored Pantone 1615) squirts from his
southern port, he grasps his phone with his
tiny hands and unleashes yet another
Twitter covfefe that leaves the world
reeling.

The next time you see Donnie and gauge his level of anger, you might want to think about what type of stool he has just passed. It can't be fun for him to live with the threat of sixes and sevens leaving him awash in excrement — nor is it fun for the rest of the world forced to live in fear under his constant shit stream. We have all heard the saying "if it's yellow, let it mellow" and Donnie, as we know, loves yellow, particularly golden yellow; it's the color of his logo, hair, and skin. But nothing about this man will ever mellow, so instead we'll focus on and adopt the second part of the rule: if it's brown, flush it down.

Holy Shit! He's Our President?

"So what if he's a shit? He's our shit!" say the toothy woodsmen from Deliverance County, Georgia. Donald cooked up a casserole of coal miners, swamp language, and Mexican rapists and has served it up on the American flag, promising he'd make America great again, make us powerful again, proud to be an American again. He'll drain that swamp, build a wall, bill the Mexicans, bring manufacturing back, and in no time flat, we'll be digging up lumps of coal again...just like grandpa used to.

To those proud and disappointed white men, I have a message: Sit down, take a deep breath. Inhale. Exhale. Inhale again. I am sorry to inform you that you've been sold a crock of shit.

Those manufacturing jobs are never coming back unless you and thousands like you want to survive on fifty cents an hour until you succumb to black lung disease. Mexico is not going to pay for the wall.

Trump has spent his entire life in the brackish green waters of a moneyed swamp where palms get greased and bankers live by the words "don't ask, don't tell." Just look at who benefits from his presidency: the rich ("We were rich as shit before, and now we're even richer!") and corporations ("He lets us shit in our own backyard and yours!).

Yet Donnie doesn't give two shits about the poor folk who believed in him and his promises and voted him into office. You were hornswoggled again. He pledged bigger tax refunds, yet most are realizing their checks will be smaller than before. And he's not finished rewarding his loyal base yet. The schools and hospitals in your communities may be shut, or their funding may be cut and redirected into the coffers of his rich cronies. Your water supply may be next, but don't be worried, just figure out how you're going to break the news to your wife and kids. It'll be okay. The family can hightail it down to the river whenever nature calls. Meanwhile, ex-

President Trump will be hanging out poolside in Riyadh. You won't see his sheiks, and I assure you, he won't hear your shrieks.

Here's whom Trump befriends: billionaires, strongmen, wall builders, welfare profiteers, river polluters, bottom feeders, Kanye West, and any other crazy willing to pat him on the back and say he's terrific.

Here's whom Trump beshits: his supporters. Oh, the shame of being shat on! It must be very, very hard to simply accept it, wipe it off, and move on. Denial comes far more easily: How much sweeter it is to say, "You don't understand" or "You're totally wrong" than it is to swallow your pride. How salty it must be to admit, "You're right and I was wrong." So instead, folks dig their heels in, hold their positions, and marinate in manure. And that's exactly where we are today: waist-deep in Trumpshit, taking sides against each other as we stew in its putrid juices.

Millions of people were taken in by Trump's appearance, impressed by his height and his tower, fooled by his fake resume and phony university, and envious of the many notches on his bedpost. But none of these mean shit; they impart no power.

Whilst physically tall, Trump is dwarfed by other world leaders. We don't need to see his college transcripts to know that he's an intellectual midget; this shit-for-brains is positively Lilliputian next to Germany's Angela Merkel, who wrote her Ph.D. thesis on quantum chemistry then worked as a scientist. When the Berlin Wall fell, she got involved in democratic politics, rising to become her country's chancellor for three terms. Merkel's been referred to as the world's most powerful woman and the de facto leader of Europe, and with her quiet authority, has earned the respect of both allies and opponents – except from Donnie, whose emotions are as stunted as his brainpower. Time and again when he's not center stage, and especially when in the presence of accomplished women, our dumbshit toddler-in-chief tosses insults, tantrums, and even the occasional object.

Donnie is a midget concealed in an outsized body. Imagine for a second that somehow Trump and Putin experience a body swap and Putin is transposed out of his 5'7" frame and gains eight inches in Trump's. Who's the giant and who's the pygmy? Does mere height define might? For clarity's sake, I'll offer another vision, one in which the leaders of Mother Russia and America the Beautiful trade places for one vacation. It's easy enough to picture Putin driving a golf cart at the Trump National Golf Club in Bedminster, New Jersey. But Trump in Siberia, shirtless and astride a horse? Inconceivable!

I'm not saying that to succeed, a leader must be an intellectual giant or a strong man (or a strongman). But leaders on the world's stage have strengths, steel, and accomplishments. Meaningful pursuits. Donnie has none of these. His proudest accomplishment is stamping his name on things in big gold letters; his only talent is his mastery of bullshit; his long-term pursuit is of long-legged fashion models.

What about his deal-making skills? Aren't they an accomplishment? By now, it should be clear to everyone that he has none. Nada. Zilch. Bravado might carry a session at the craps table, but it's no substitute for the facts, diplomacy, and persistence needed at the world's negotiating table. It's impossible to debate complex issues without historical context, without an understanding of the others' positions, and without the ability, patience, and temperament to reason with them. You may as well stick your tongue out or your middle finger up — and this is exactly what Donnie does. He is the clown of the international arena who prefers love-ins with dictators like Kim Jong-un and President Putin to the messy long-term toil of the United Nations or NATO. A buffoon who prefers snap decisions to labored thinking. A dipshit or shitbar who trusts his gut when most politicians know that what you feel down there is mainly gas.

Facts remain a pesky annoyance to Trump because they contradict his claim of the moment — that the climate isn't changing, Obama wasn't born in America, or Putin didn't interfere with the election. But for other world leaders seated at the grown-ups' table, facts are, in fact, table stakes, yet Donnie shows up each time with empty pockets and even emptier threats. They know he's a fuckwit, that there's no deal to be done and no conversation to be had, so until POTUS 46 shows up, they're left to make small talk around Donnie as he grins and eats the extra scoop of soft-serve, chocolate-covered shit heaped upon his gold-leaf plate.

If a digitized recording of Trump's voice while rallying his supporters could be stripped of his anger and sales-pitchiness, you'd instantly hear him for what he is at his core: a chattering gibbon, the smallest of apes, and known for being noisy and territorial. Donnie's sentences make no

more sense than a shitgibbon's — they are
literally nonsense, words that have been
chopped up and heaped on a plate like
Caesar salad. Except Trump is no Caesar,
but he is a seizer: of media minutes, of
common sense, of our future.

Shit At Business

Tomes have been written about how poor a businessman The Don really is. I will not wade up shit creek into that feculent marsh but simply stress here that Donnie's maniacal desire for self-promotion, self-aggrandizement, and exaggeration have muddied his record with dirty squirties. He's spent and lost billions but largely shoved his losses to banks and bonds. Netted out, he's probably made the same as your average mailman, except that his father gave Donnie $400 million before he even started his route. This is not the work of a titan like Warren Buffet, Bill Gates, or Howard Schulz. Drop the "-an" from "titan" for Donnie's true size: he's just a bit of a tit.

The Trump Organization today is a triumph of marketing over taste, of gold lettering, golf courses, and teeth-grinding gaudiness. If we wanted a hotelier as president, we could have looked to the Marriott family who have many times more locations, employees, and years of experience, and are renowned worldwide for their commitment to ethical leadership. If we wanted a successful businessman as president, we could have picked Mitt Romney back in 2012. We've ended up with not a businessman as president, but a performer who formerly played a businessman on TV. An actor. Is it really all that difficult to differentiate between an actor and the characters they play on screen?

When we watch *Top Gun*, we see Tom Cruise as Maverick, the rebellious navy aviator. As Maverick, he wins the girl and whips the Russians. The story is infantile, but we eat it up. If Cruise ran for president wearing a Maverick hat and talking about "bogeys at nine o' clock" or requesting a flyby, we'd laugh our asses off because we know he's just an actor – he can't fly or fight Russians!

When we watch *Wall Street*, we see Michael Douglas as Gordon Gekko, the venal capitalist preaching that "greed is good" and "if you need a friend, get a dog." He's a winner for sure, but a self-serving scumbag like Gordon Gekko would make a truly terrible president. Michael Douglas played other memorable characters in films like *Fatal Attraction*, *War of the Roses*, and even the title role in *The American President*. We don't presume he shares the same flaws and qualities of those characters, because he's Michael Douglas, the actor.

When we watch *The Apprentice*, we see Donald Trump, the failed businessman and self-serving scumbag playing Donald Trump, successful businessman. But the TV show isn't even about business; the mechanics and visuals of business are far too tame for reality TV, so the show morphed into a game of personal intrigues, judgments, and ultimately humiliation for the loser. Just as Tom Cruise can't fly an F-14 and Michael Douglas isn't a corporate raider, Donnie isn't a successful businessman. They're all just actors.

If you were shooting the movie *Treasure Island* and casting the role of pirate Long John Silver's parrot, you'd want a bird that talks on cue, utters funny phrases, and — more or less — sits still, claws-on-perch. So it was for Mark Burnett, the producer of *The Apprentice*. He needed a human parrot to spout lines at the right time, make the audience believe they were his own, and then applaud. Burnett found one, Donnie got the part of the parrot, and the rest is history.

The role of Donnie the Parrot was loosely scripted by the network and shaped into a half-hour slot to hold the audience's attention long enough for advertisers to sneak in intravenous messaging during commercial breaks. Like stage magicians who palm a card, the producers of *The Apprentice* timed its events to the second to make you watch the featured Ford or a pink-faced grandpa pitching pharmaceuticals. The show was the carrier, the ads the payload, and Trump's volcanic eruptions the money shot. Together, this unholy yin and

yang were injected into viewers'
bloodstreams every Thursday evening. The
American public's hearts pumped blood
around and through their brains as their
eyes drank in the spectacle of "Trump —
businessman — tough and smart."

Well, viewers may have thought that
Donnie was a wise and powerful Yoda but
they were really just there to watch trucks
pulling logs up mountains. His insults and
firings made for sassy TV, but they were
little more than training sessions that while
pharmaceuticals might kill you (if you had
certain medical preconditions), they might
make your mood better or your penis
harder, so go ask your doctor for some
right now.

Or maybe the audience didn't care,
maybe they understood that it was all
bullshit — but hell, it was kind of fun to
watch on Thursday night, wasn't it? So
millions of people tuned in to that
unmitigated swill year-in and year-out
instead of reading a good book or playing

with their kids or talking to a friend about
— well, about the real world. One way or
another, Americans got used to the concept
of Donald Trump being a businessman, not
just an actor. And at the same time, Donnie
got used to playing a businessman on TV.

Now we have an actor who thinks he's a
successful businessman because he played
one for 14 seasons and has been elected
leader of the free world. Trump, that old
shit, falls back on his old tricks because
they're the only tricks that parrot knows.
But when he finds they don't work
anymore, he flails around, hopelessly
tweeting insults, squawking "pieces of hate,
pieces of hate". Ruffling feathers and
flapping his wings so hard they knocked
things over was a big part of the master
plan, anyway.

This is the Peter Principle gone berserk:
Trump has been promoted not just to the
level of his own incompetence, but far, far
beyond it into the shitosphere. It would be
like having a school janitor run a nuclear

submarine during covert ops or dressing a truck driver in a leotard and making them the star of Cirque de Soleil. Donald Trump being president, or even acting as president, is quite possibly the worst miscasting in human history.

This poor boor is a dumb shit with no political knowledge, no political experience, and no judgment. How the hell is he supposed to function as president? Sure, there are cameras like there were on *The Apprentice*, only now he can't shout "cut" to have the producers scramble to reshoot a shitty scene. And neither can we. Little Donnie wants it to be like it was back in the old days — when the cameras loved him, all the bloopers got edited out, and the audience thought he was tough. There were no real-world consequences to the show; causing offense was part of the game, and a shag on the side was easy to find and find time for.

Now, he's cast his supporting roles with sycophants to wipe his ass perpetually clean while there are hundreds of millions of people offstage, booing. Donnie is spoon-fed his lines, but when he ad-libs people laugh at him. Just like the Trump Organization, *The Apprentice* was an autocracy — he liked it that way — but now he runs a democracy. Nancy Pelosi can roll her eyes and say no. Congress can say no. Lawmakers can say no. And so should we.

Trump sold us the dummy of an actor who'd played a businessman and wanted the leading role of president. America bought it. And now all of us pay. We pay now and we will pay later. On matters like the environment and world relations, he will set us back decades, maybe kill us. The Doomsday Clock — a symbolic measure of danger in this nuclear age — was moved forward 30 seconds in 2018 and remains at two minutes to midnight, but Trump claims it doesn't even exist.

To Trump, all is well in the world so long as he can watch the sprinklers on his golf courses and hit send on his Twitter

account while Republican working-class
voters get used to sub-subsistence wages
that will never, ever, ever rise. The sea will
rise however, and the snowpack will shrink,
and sooner or later there will be a water or
food crisis that threatens billions of people.
If you have a lot of barbed wire, well-fed
and well-armed guards, and military
preparations, you'll probably be fine. You
won't be able to play golf, though, because
the fairways will become deserts once
there's no water for the sprinklers. And
you won't be living at Mar-a-Lago unless
you own a canoe.

Shitty President

It's one thing to be a shit in your
private life: a shit that fucks around on
your wives, a shit that cons working people
out of their money, a shit that talks shit
about anyone who disagrees with or
criticizes their shit. It's quite another to
stuff all those shitty flaws into an
overflowing sack of shit and carry it into
the White House.

You'd think that looking up at portraits
of the great men on the wall or at bronze
busts of world leaders in the Oval Office
might bring out the best in our president.
Instead, it flushes out the worst in him.
Instead, Donnie bristles. Instead of giving a
shit about the office of the president, he's
going to do it his way and disregard and
disrespect the rules. He'll dodge the stiff
arm of the law and accept a high-five or a
slap on the wrist later. He'll keep
disinforming, misinforming, lying, and always
remaining a moving target, because a
moving target is harder to hit. Obama's

portrait must be the most grating to him. Donnie seems obsessed with the size of Obama's sand castles and has a childish need to stamp them down and build his own — but his castles must be bigger and taller, with moats and a wall. Did Obama's speech about Trump at the White House Correspondents' Dinner in 2011 really humiliate Don so badly that it motivated him to run? Is all of this shit, piss, and corruption merely about avenging Barack's insults?

Whether you love the smell of his shit or hate it, one thing is certain: Donnie will never unite this country. He gets a lot of headlines and attention but gets very little done. Even Trump supporters must concede that Donnie is never going to bring Democrats (who, let's not forget, won the majority of votes in 2016 and 2018) to the negotiating table.

This autocrat's agenda was doomed from the start by the animosity he engendered among Democrats in Congress. There will always be Republicans and Democrats, and without compromise from both sides, there can be no meaningful progress. Donnie isn't smart enough to know that the bull in the china shop achieves nothing but broken crockery. And all that's left behind him is a collection of shards: jagged, useless, and dangerous. The shards will have to be picked up or tossed to his successor, but some of their damage will be impossible to reverse. Look at pictures of ruined Raqqa. Who won there? Nobody. Don't tear down the house in D.C. just because the other side is taking over. In four or eight years, you will — in turn — be taking it back from them.

This president has no sense of history or his place in it. He cannot see himself from a third-party perspective. He has no sense of objectivity, no ability to carefully weigh opposing points of view, no ability to express himself in more than 280 characters. He is a dunderhead surrounded by cawing crows. Sycophants applaud him. Fux News kneads his flabby back. The rest of the world's roughly seven billion people (I've subtracted Russia) roll their eyes and shake their heads.

Donnie knows less about politics than any other president in history. He knows about hotel wallpaper and sand traps. He doesn't know how great bargains are made and broken; he knows great cons. He has a moron's point of view about climate change and the environment. All the proof he needs is right in front of his eyes: Florida is sunny and his fairways are green.

This country needs a leader with relevant experience, morals, and the ability to reach across the aisle and smile and talk. The last election offered candidates with these qualities: John Kasich, Jeb Bush, Joe Biden. They had relevant experience. They could have forged consensus. Hilary Clinton and Bernie Sanders could not. Ted Cruz would not. And Donald Trump cannot. Can you imagine Donnie giving Hillary a conciliatory handshake? Or Cruz complimenting Sanders with sincerity?

Folks, Donnie won anyway.

Yes, he did. Despite the bile and cheese of his campaign, despite the people he shat on, despite his raccoon eyes and orange skin, he did win the Electoral College and yes, he is our president. On that amazing evening of November 8th, 2016, he broke the mold, and as he unclenched his fist the possibility of greatness was right there in the open palm of his little hand — right there! He could have brought Democrats and Republicans together since he had no real roots in either party. He could have knocked heads and led us forward. Instead, he succumbed to instinct and looked for conflict. He clenched his fist again and threw a left punch so hard that it disappeared up his own ass, his knuckles plowing all the way up to his sigmoid colon. When he pulled out his steaming shitty knuckles, he smelled his fist, and went cat shit crazy. Two-and-a-half-years later, Bill Barr comes in to clean up.

Donnie is only and all about winning.
He didn't give governing a second thought
until election night, and he isn't smart
enough to realize that ruling is different
than running. He still sees the same fist but
now with a presidential stamp, the same
microphone but in front of Congress, and is
the same old shit but now he spews it from
Airforce One and 1600 Pennsylvania
Avenue. My God was he wrong.

All of the qualities that got him there —
the swagger, the crudeness, the lust for and
love of controversy, the desire to hog the
camera — all these qualities are, in fact,
liabilities and will eventually poison him. His
delusion is that he believes he is the hero of
his self-created crises, the strongman, the
visionary. Instead, he is the crank, the dope,
the lump of shit.

He does not yet understand that most
of America has a gag reflex, and while it
has been delayed, it will still yet cough him
up like a furball, and the rain will wash
this knotty, matted yellow hair though the

court system and down the drain. His little band of misfit friends will burrow into their holes and hide in their own frass.

Americans chose Donnie because too many have watched so much reality television and so many shitty three-act movies that they've bought the idea that a highlight reel makes the actor makes the man. Let me tell you: Everyone has a highlight reel, and no one should be measured by it. You shouldn't judge a politician by a funny or fatal tweet, by a bad debate performance, or by a single off-color remark. You should judge them by their years of legislative grind, by the depth of their thinking, by their connections to those who bitterly oppose them (even the powerful must move adversaries, too), and by their ability to achieve consensus and then to lead.

The biggest shouter is often the biggest loser. The biggest bully won't be able to get much done and will put the backs up of half the population. Only a dunce like

Trump believes a president hands a carved tablet to The Hill and says, "Make it so!"

Let's also not forget this guy lost the popular vote...by millions. Then lied that he didn't, then invented an inquiry to prove that he didn't, then when it concluded that he did, he simply ignored it.

But in the end, we all lost.

Donnie will continue to shit sniffle at the Constitution without realizing he should actually read it. Or act on it. Maybe he'll raise his hind leg and piss on it or take it in his jaws and worry it and gnaw on it like a dog. Or maybe he'll just reprint it on yellowed paper and title it The Trump Constitution in gilt lettering with a burlap bow and pretend it's a diploma from Trump University.

Future generations will not understand (nor will they care) why Donnie was fixated on border fencing; they will live in a world where Miami is underwater, the environment has been savaged and ravaged, and the food chain has been destroyed. It will be hard for them to fathom how our national psyche would have chosen this ignorant shit in the first place, and why, oh why, the good men and women of the Republican Party would continue to dance to this Pied Piper's tune even as it led them over a cliff.

When King Shit finally leaves the White House, forensic cleaners will use industrial-grade chemicals and toothbrushes to clean every yellow hair, every fleck of brown skin, and every trickle of sickly sweat off the Resolute desk and the carpet beneath it, then expunge the smell, the shit stains, and the skid marks from his chair.

"Being president of this country is all about character," said President Andrew Shepard in The American President. Our president doesn't have a single ounce of it. Donnie is the *Limax maximus* of American politics – a long black slug with horny tentacles, secreting a glistening trail of slime that fouls everything behind him.

Shitty Human

Our president is a shit person. There are no externalities in Trump's world, there's just him and his needs: his pockets, his belly, his penis, his fame. That's it.

I won't linger long on this subject because it has already been covered by reams and tomes and yet Donnie's still here, smirking away at the shit papers every morning.

It's said that charity begins at home and Donnie is certainly a big believer — so long as the good cause enriches Donald J. Trump. When it comes to his own personal giving, he's completely full of shit, making grandiose claims but rarely opening his checkbook. However, if someone sets up a charity on his behalf, Little Donnie is happy to break open its piggy bank and spend the money on "wonderful charities": namely, himself. As reported by The New York Times, the attorney general of the state of New York found that The Trump

Foundation worked tirelessly for his benefit in "a shocking pattern of illegality," including defending lawsuits against Trump, bidding to win a portrait of himself for twenty thousand dollars, and engaging in political activity.

The Don is a shit husband. He marries, purportedly fucks around, and trades in older models for newer ones. His 1977 marriage to model Ivana Zelnickova ended in a train wreck of recriminations and embarrassment after he began an affair with 26 year-old Marla Maples, a former beauty queen turned actress. Rather than break this news gently to his wife — the mother of his first three children and an executive with The Trump Organization — this allegedly philandering shit-slinger planted stories in the press so Ivana would get the message. She did, and they divorced.

He went on to marry mistress Maples, but only did so after she gave birth to their daughter. When he divorced her six years later, he left Maples to raise Tiffany alone

— he's a shit father as well as a shit husband. Marriage isn't a promise to be kept, so why shouldn't he cut and run? Here in his third term as a shit husband, Donnie truly proved that practice makes perfect, marrying fashion model Melania Knauss, 24 years his junior, in 2005. In less than a year, the future first lady was pregnant, and by the time she had baby Barron, it is alleged that her not-so-dutiful husband was doing the nasty with both Karen McDougal and Stormy Daniels. Beautiful — it is possible that while Melania was nursing his infant son, Donnie was plowing a new furrow (or two), dropping his seed, washing his hands, then heading home for a goodnight kiss from the wife.

Donnie is a very experienced and rapid-fire liar. It's probably one of his deftest and most practiced skills, and his current pace of around five lies per day is breaking all presidential records. Being the "most" and "best" really matters to him; a spot in Guinness World Records will undoubtedly be his and will stand for centuries.

He's a fraud who preyed upon — and profited from — the dreams of ordinary folk. Using high-pressure tactics, Trump University persuaded thousands of "students" that its seminars would share the secrets to succeeding in real estate. From 2005 to 2010, the shit businessman bilked people of their hard-earned money and gave them worthless pablum in return. He finally settled the class-action lawsuits for fraud perpetrated by his fake university for $25 million.

He cheats as easily as he breathes through his shitnose. "To say 'Donald Trump cheats' is like saying 'Michael Phelps swims'," writes Rick Riley in his book *Commander in Cheat: How Golf Explains Trump.* "He cheats at the highest level. He cheats when people are watching him, and he cheats when they aren't."

But Donnie's a very, very dim bulb. He perpetrates the myth of being smart to cover the fact that he's thick as shit. His vocabulary is mainly limited to monosyllabic and disyllabic words. His primitive attempts at sentences often contain no verbs, or if they do contain verbs, the verbs don't agree with the subjects. His conditional sentences are often incomplete. He overuses superlatives and exclamation marks, classic symptoms of severe insecurity. He waffles, speaks in tautologies, and contradicts assertions he himself has just made. Basically, Donnie has an incomplete grasp of English language, syntax, and usage. He's a bit of dunce. He compensates by making false claims with fierce force one after the other, rather like a water cannon hosing a protester.

Impious. If you hear Mr. Trump talking about religion, you will intuitively understand that he's not religious. Not even a smidgen. Words like sacrifice, humble, love, generosity, confession, forgiveness, and grace do not describe the Don. More accurate might be words like pride, greed, lust, envy, glutton, wrath and sloth — i.e. the seven deadly sins. Christians who wear "What

Would Jesus Do" bracelets should pause for a second and ask themselves this: "What would Jesus make of this man, his morals, and his behavior?" I pray that they consider that question carefully.

Petty, vindictive, inflexible, bigoted, unfocused, ill-disciplined, arrogant...the list goes on and on and on. Rex Tillerson was a "world class player" on the way in and "dumb as a rock" on the way out. Steve Bannon was "tough and smart" on the way in but "sloppy Steve" who had "lost his mind" on the way out – hold on, I need the smelling salts. The putrid odor of this shitty human has crept up my nose and is headed down the back of my throat.

Why, oh why, would America want such a lowlife as president? Why would America want someone who eschews intellect for instinct, someone who can't spell or even speak correctly, someone who can't control their own penis? There's a lot of detritus in this world. But never before has someone not fit to shovel shit become president of the United States.

Scrape The Trumpshit Off Your Shoes

Where I grew up, walking in the fields left you with a good deal of mud and shit caked on your boots. You couldn't track that filth inside unless you wanted a cuffing from mother, so we had a boot scraper by the door. You'd lift each leg and drag each boot against the cast iron several times to scrape all that shit off, tug off your boots, then head inside. This kept our house clean. It really is a shame we let a president with such filthy boots tramp shit all over the White House.

So how do we scrape off the Trumpshit? The answer is simple: Elections are our modern-day boot-scraper. Elections give each of us a vote and a voice.

Elections often have a bumpy approach followed by a white-knuckle landing, but after we've all filed in and out of the voting booths, there's no difference between

a quiet vote and a loud vote, an angry vote
and a content vote — all the X's are
counted. Despite all the Trumpian nonsense
about electoral fraud and illegal voting in
2018, there was none. All the votes were
counted.

But to get to the ballot, we have to
first get through the campaign, and the
media will — for its own purposes —
guarantee that we fly through a veritable
shitstorm. Rational and balanced arguments
simply do not maximize eyeballs or page
views. Horror, comedy, and anger do. So
you can be sure that any modern American
election will be frightening, hilarious, and
truly revolting. The politicos on both sides
will demonize and weaponize their
opponents. Exaggeration will become our
daily diet, poured on our cornflakes and
put on our pasta. Every day a million little
clips will be assembled to make us hate the
other side, make our blood pressure rise,
and raise our bile.

How the media loves to cover the

loudest and craziest of voices! There's not much news — and no ad revenue — in reporting on reasonable, quietly opinionated, happy people. By following the whack-jobs and extremists instead, the media pleases sympathizers, drives opponents crazy, and sends ratings sky-high all in the name of covering the facts fairly (of course). Whenever it can, it must draw contrast — stark contrast — by labeling points of view as ditzy, disruptive, or dangerous. It's part of the media's daily fight to get their own "fair" share of attention from viewers, and the competition is fanged and fierce: user-generated content from desperados seeking attention, kitten videos, free porn, salvation preachers, plus all the traditional staid content like news, comedy, and drama. If politics turns you off, you can always watch a tan, ugly, fat creep have sex with an insatiable blond, or a few mewing kittens, or a preacher pounding his fist and casting out Satan, or a documentary on a depraved serial killer.

We are long, long past the point where

you turn to the media for facts, because the fact is, Big Media must sell the viewer every single day...and sell hard. If there's no sizzle, there's no steak; there are simply too many saucy places to go. Very few people read balanced, boring news. To stay relevant and not lose viewers, the media has little choice but to stir up the hornet's nest and sting a few people. They are selling emotion, not facts, these days.

Unfortunately, the demolition of the traditional press has lobotomized America and doomed us to a land of listicles and bearded ladies. And there's only one way to shut this circus down (which we'll never do): Stop watching video news. The facial expressions of pundits, the hosts' contrived skepticism, the pitch and frenzy of their voices...every detail from the tits to the testosterone to the perfectly white teeth has been designed to manipulate your emotions. You might think that watching is little more than a guilty pleasure, but in fact it's a drug — it's destructive and it's highly addictive. The media doesn't care about you or your well-being, it doesn't care whether it's distorting the underlying message. It wants your eyeballs.

Every moment we spend watching broadcast video gives our brains a moment to collect dust, or even to rust a little. Before you know it, your brain will be full of cobwebs and your memory crawling with spiders. One evening you'll be staring at Fux News, a slack-jawed sheep nodding and listening to automatons bleating propaganda. And the very next evening? You'll do the same again. All those hours spent, brain on idle, wasting your life away. All those hours lost to Big Media's intoxicating cocktail: three shots of outrage, one of common sense, with a dash of humor, and automobile and drug ads on the side.

So instead, switch off your TV or even better, toss it away. Log out of Facebook where your idiot relative proudly posts a selfie taken while making a peace sign in front of a charging lion. Eliminate video news completely and get the gift which keeps on giving...time. There are so many more productive things you can spend it on.

1. Spend time with your kids or your parents or your loved ones. Walk with them, talk with them, or take them somewhere they've never been and remember the wonder of experiencing something new, something real. Remember what it's like to actually participate in life, rather than merely viewing others doing it.

2. Talk to your friends, preferably in person, one-on-one. Put down your phone and engage in conversation. Tell them what you're thinking, share your position on issues you care about, ask where they stand, and find out what worries them.

3. Write to your actual members of Congress instead of commenting on websites frequented by the lunatic fringe. Contact the people who need your vote and who actually need to listen to your voice. It's pointless to pick a fight with surrogates of Alex Jones and their oily ilk, who live only

to keep conspiracy theories alive.

4. Encourage people to vote. Okay, maybe not the people who spout Trumplove. But it's important to democracy that everyone — everyone! — participates. Abstention is not good. Voting activates a muscle, promotes and provokes conversation, and attaches a mooring line through time back to election day. We must make a habit of voting — for our own good in discharging our personal responsibility and commitment to civility as much as for our vote itself. The day after an election we can converse with others and be proud we participated (no matter who won), rather than sit home in silent protest.

5. Read. Then read more. And keep on reading, reading, reading. The process of reading a book is the polar opposite of watching TV. Instead of checking your brain as you drop into a chair and let the media flood into it, read. It engages your brain. Pulling words from the page one-by-one, absorbing them, and processing them feeds

both the brain and the soul. Read around
subjects you ought to know more about.
The truth is this: few of us know much
about anything, and the quicker we are to
admit it, the quicker we can start to learn.

6. Discount or ignore the gibbering of
our shitgibbon president. It's all scrapple
picked up from Fux News, hearsay,
sycophants, and the odd inspiration from a
stray synapse that recalls a childhood
prejudice. Ignore it all.

Look yourself in the mirror and say,
"Instead of watching, I will think, I will
talk, I will vote." Video is the medium of
Trumpoma: the cancer that is Trump. We
can't physically resect this tumor, but we
can deprive it of our attention — the fuel it
needs to spread — and in doing so, have a
better chance of staying healthy and sane
ourselves.

Take heed of my namesake George
Orwell's warning, "If you want a picture of
the future, imagine a boot stamping on a

human face — forever." This is Brother
Trump, this is video journalism, and this is
where America is allowing itself to be led.

Goodbye Shit!

In summary, Mr. President, you are a shit and you give us the shits. We're sick of your horseshit. Shit-sack Day is coming, your time is almost up, and you're shit out of luck. Get ready to pack up your shit and shit-addle back to Florida. Holy shit – 1600 Pennsylvania will stop being a shithouse and become the White House again!

Donnie, once you're gone, you can stay shit-faced if you want; your spray-on tan won't bother us. You can keep being a shit to your wife – not our business. You can keep doing the same old shit and put gaudy gold lettering up on your shitscrapers. We don't care. Just leave us, shithead, leave us alone. Give Washington a break from your perpetual shitstorm. We'll be happy as pigs in shit because we'll have a paddle and we won't be up shit creek anymore. We'll have someone in power who actually gives a shit. Someone who doesn't have shitfits. Or dipshits in their Cabinet. No shit, Sherlock!

Yes, we've got a lot of shit to do and you can help us all by wiping the fecal treacle off your chair behind the Resolute desk, taking your crock of shit elsewhere, and shitting the door behind you. You Sir, were, are, and will always be a total shit. Goodbye, shit!

The Shittery: A Lexicon of Modern Trumpspeak

Donnie's shit so permeates every aspect of our lives that he is turning America into a total shittery, a place so muddied by browns that even familiar shit can be unrecognizable. This Shittery will help you get your bearings in our Trump-centered world, providing explanations for how and why the shit truly hits the fan. Just below it are some un-shitty bonus definitions.

We welcome suggestions, revisions, and insertions. Email paul@paulorwell.com

AIN'T GOT / Ain't got shit on me: Trump's position on Russia

ALL OVER / Shit all over: Donnie trolls latest target

BAD / Bad shit: Trump not happy

BANG / Bang like a shithouse door in a gale: door noise as fired staffers exit

BARR / (i) complete idiot (ii) current Attorney General

BE- / Beshits: soil with presidential

excrement

BEAR / Does a bear shit in the woods?: Does Trump fabricate facts?

BEAT / Beat the shit out of: punishment meted out to dissenters at Trump rally

BED / Shit the bed: Donnie tweets in the morning

BETWEEN / Stuck between a shit and a sweat: Republicans facing re-election

BIRD / Stick that bottom lip out any further and a bird might shit on it: Trump pouts at Merkel

BRAINS / Shit for brains: matter inside Trump's cranium

BREATH/ Shit breath: Donnie needs Tic Tacs

BRICK / Shit a brick: start building The Wall

BRICKHOUSE / Built like a brick shithouse: able to withstand caravans

BULL / Bullshit: only language Trump speaks fluently

BURGER / Shitburger: dinner ordered for college football championship teams

CANNED / Shitcanned: fired while literally sitting on toilet, e.g. Rex Tillerson

CAT / Slicker than catshit on linoleum: Sarah Huckabee Sanders

CAT- / cat-shit crazy: DJT after unfair segment on Fux News

CHEAP / Cheap shit: Trump-branded rubbish meant to evoke wealth

CHOCOLATE-COVERED / Chocolate-covered shit: sweeten it up, swallow it down!

CREEK / Up shit creek: our environment at present; both water and climate not good

CROCK / Crock of shit: Barr's summary of Mueller report

-DADDLE / Shitdaddle: run away from the president

DEEP / Deep shit: Trump thinks for a second

DIP / Dipshit: stock market goes down after a Trump tweet

DOG / Dogshit: women Donnie finds unattractive

DUMB / Dumb shit: Donald J. Trump

EAT / Eat shit: work for POTUS 45

-ERATI / Shitterati: celebrities attending the 2016 inauguration

FACED / Shit-faced: Trump after applying tanning lotion

FAN / When the shit hits the fan: Trump bodyguard punches protester

FIT / Have a shit-fit: Donnie reads bad press

FLIES / Like flies on shit: religious right visits White House

FOR BRAINS / Shit-for-brains: Tillerson's assessment of Donnie

FRIGHTEN / Frighten the shit out of: Russian pee-tapes

FUCKING / Fucking shit: Trump has extramarital sex

FULL OF / Full of shit: 2+ days since Trump had bowel movement

GET / Get one's shit together: prepare for deposition

GIBBON / Shitgibbon: Trump explaining himself

GIVE / Give a shit (or two shits): POTUS 45 does not

GIVE SOMEONE / Give someone shit: be

Donald Trump

GOT / Got the shits: Trump gets letter from the Southern District of New York

GRIN / shit-eating grin: Donnie after Mueller report

HAPPENS / Shit happens: Trump's work philosophy

HEAD / Shithead: golden hair on pate

HOLE / Shithole: any country in Africa

HOLY / Holy shit: The Pope; Donnie calls him "disgraceful"

HORSE / Horseshit: Trump University coursework

HOT / Hot shit: (i) Trump under a sunbed; (ii) attractive female to Donnie

HOUSE / Shithouse: Mar-a-Lago

HUMAN / Shitty human: Donnie

IGNORANT / Ignorant shit: Stephen Miller

IN YOUR OWN BACKYARD / Shit in your own backyard: pro-Trump rally in your home city

JACK / Jack-shit: what Donnie gives to charity

KING / King Shit: Donald Trump

LIST / Shit list: (i) Democrats who annoy Donnie; (ii) loyalists who contradict him

LITTLE / Little shit: Marco

LOT OF _ TO DO / Lot of shit to do: many attorneys to speak to

LUCK / Shit out of luck: Trump's casinos close down

LUMP OF / Lump of shit: Donnie

MEAN / Mean shit: (i) Robert Mueller; (ii) lie

NASTY / Soft as shit and twice as nasty: Trump in bed

NO / No shit: Trump out of office

NOSE / Shitnose: head up Donald's rectum, e.g. Barr, Bolton, Jared

OH / Oh shit!: realization on waking that it isn't a dream - Donnie is POTUS

OLD / Old shit: Donald Trump

-OSPHERE / Shitosphere: within farting distance of DJT

OUT OF LUCK / see Luck

PACK UP / Pack up your shit: electoral result of 2020

PANTS / Shit one's pants: defeated by

Nancy Pelosi

PAPER / Shitpaper: Washington Post, New York Times

PIECE / Piece of shit: any Democrat in Trump's eyes

PIG / Happy as a pig in shit: Stephen Miller

PILE / Pile of shit: inbound mail to 1600 Pennsylvania Avenue

PISS AND CORRUPTION / Shit, piss, and corruption: Donnie's daily routine

PUSHING UPHILL / Pushing shit uphill: reasoning with Donnie

REMEMBER / Can't remember shit: Trump under oath

RICH AS / Rich as shit: as rich as Donnie, i.e. not that rich at all

-SACK / Shit-sack: Donnie's physique

SACK DAY / Shit-sack Day: holiday celebrated after Trump loses, retires, or is impeached

SACK OF / Sack of shit: Donnie's physique

SAME OLD / Same old shit: another day in the Oval Office for Donnie

SANDWICH / Shit sandwich: squashed by Donnie on the mattress

SAUNA / Shit sauna: Trump's tanning bed

-SCRAPER / Shitscraper (i) Trump Tower at 725 5th Avenue, New York; (ii) metal bar to remove shit from boots

SCENE / Shitty scene: Donnie explaining to wife where he has been and with whom

SHERLOCK / No shit, Sherlock: Donnie to Mueller

SHINOLA / Know the difference between shit and Shinola: Trump doesn't

SHOOT / Shoot the shit: apprehend illegal immigrant with gun

SHOVEL / Shovel shit: hold press conference for Donnie

SHOW / Shitshow: *The Apprentice*

SNIFFLE / Shit sniffle: subtle sign that Trump's parking a turd

SOFT / Soft as shit: Donald Trump without an election/erection

SQUIRREL / Nuttier than squirrel shit:

Ben Carson

STACK / Didn't know you could stack shit that high: (eventual) realization of Rex Tillerson

STAIN / Shit stain: self-tanning lotion on clothes

STINK / His shit doesn't stink: Trump guarantees it

STIR UP / Stir up shit: send a tweet

STIRRER / Shit-stirrer: New York Times

STOMPERS / Shit stompers: supporters at Trump rallies

STORM / Shit storm: Hurricane Maria

SWEATS / Shit sweats: what congressional Republicans feel when defending their man

TAKE / Take shit from: remove papers from Resolute desk

THE / The shits: (i) feeling after listening to Donnie; (ii) the Cabinet

-TER / Shitter: place where Donnie tweets

THICK / Thick as shit: born with Trump's intelligence

THROW / Throw shit against the wall:

manhandle a protester

TICKET / Shit ticket: Trump + Pence for 2020

TON / Shit ton: large number two

TOO OLD / Too old for this shit: Steven Bannon

TOUGH / Tough shit: President Putin

TRUMP- / Trumpshit: pure presidential excrement

TURNED TO / Turned to shit: Donnie touched it

UP TO YOUR NECK IN / Up to your neck in shit: investigating Donnie, e.g. New York district attorney

WEIRD / Weird shit: POTUS 43's opinion of POTUS 45's inauguration speech

WENT OUT / Went out to shit and the hog ate him: staffer went to see POTUS and got fired

WRITES ITSELF / This shit writes itself: ink from Steven Miller's pen

ZERO / Zero shits given: Trump aid to Puerto Rico

Un-Shitty Appendix to The Shittery

Definitions of terms that don't contain the letters "shit" but are no less shitty:

BROTHER TRUMP / gold-seeking autocrat who insults and offends; incorrigibles love Brother Trump

COPROPHAGIA / to eat shit (literally)

DECLARATION OF ELIMINATION / POTUS 45's Inaugural Speech

DONNIE THE PARROT / star of *The Apprentice*

FRASS / excrement of insects

FUX NEWS / News for dumb fux

LIMAX MAXIMUS / horny slug, e.g. Donnie

PETER PRINCIPLE / Trump's phallus-driven organizational philosophy

TRUMP CONSTITUTION / 280 characters to include words terrific, tremendous, and loser

TRUMPOMA / the cancer of being Trump and the effect of Trump on U.S.

TRUMPOSAUR / political dinosaur soon
to be extinct

TRUMPLOVE / proles' attitude to Big T

TRUMPOCRACY / it's my way or the
highway

Acknowledgments

The Bristol Stool School and Illustrations.

The History of Shit by Dominique LaPorte which was an inspiration.

My thanks to B, K, K, C and J.